ArgoInk

Color Three

Illustrated by

Chris Argo

ISBN-13: 978-1475239393
ISBN-10: 1475239394

http://www.ArgoInk.com

To my Father

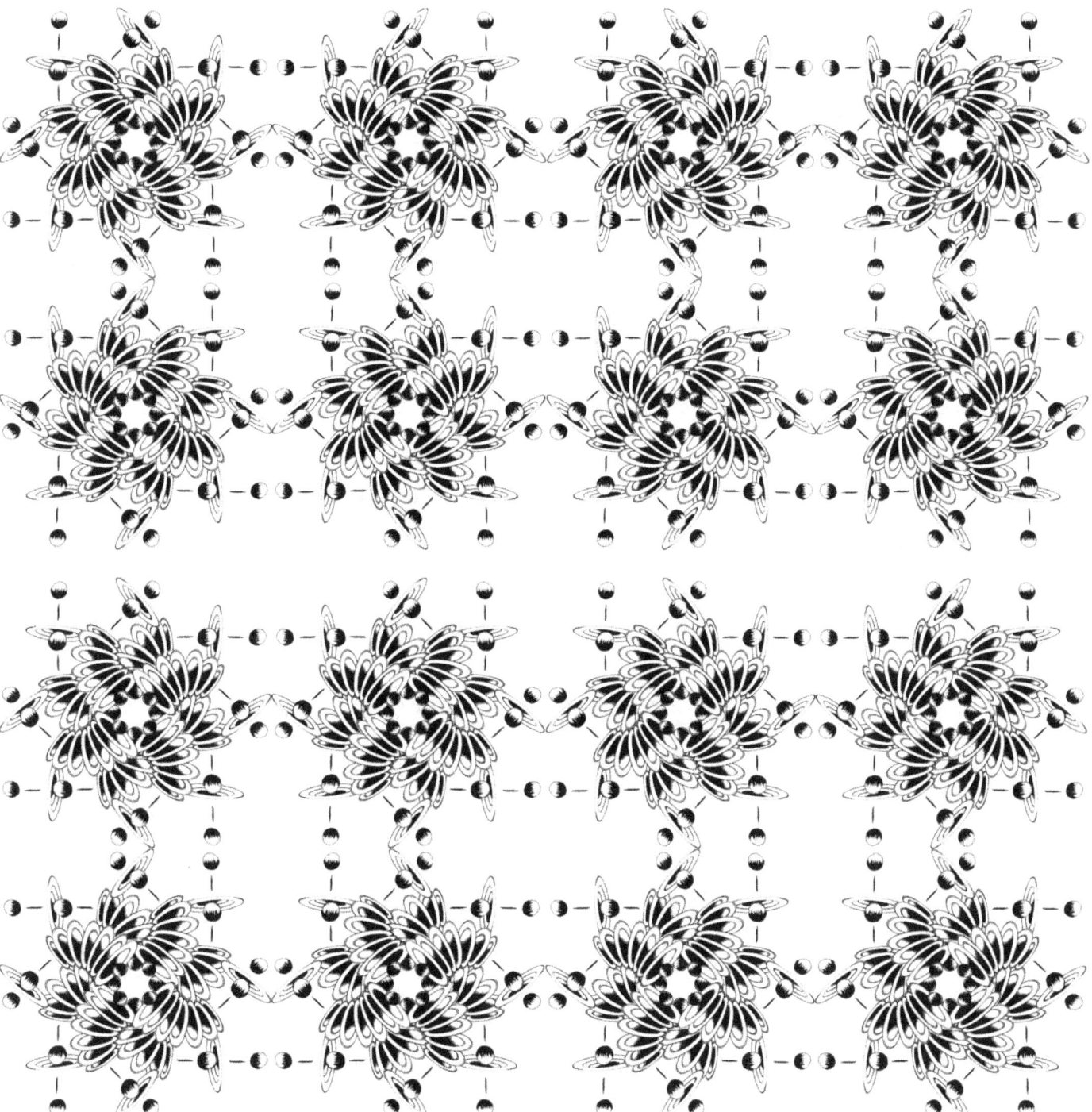

"Our deepest fear is not that we are inadequate. Our deepest fear is that we are powerful beyond measure. It is our light, not our darkness that most frightens us. We ask ourselves, who am I to be brilliant, gorgeous, talented, fabulous? Actually, who are you NOT to be? You are a child of God. Your playing small does not serve the world. There is nothing enlightened about shrinking so that other people won't feel insecure around you. We are all meant to shine, as children do. We were born to make manifest the glory of God that is within us. It's not just in some of us; it's in everyone. And as we let our own light shine, we unconsciously give other people permission to do the same. As we are liberated from our own fear, our presence automatically liberates others."

-- Nelson Mandela

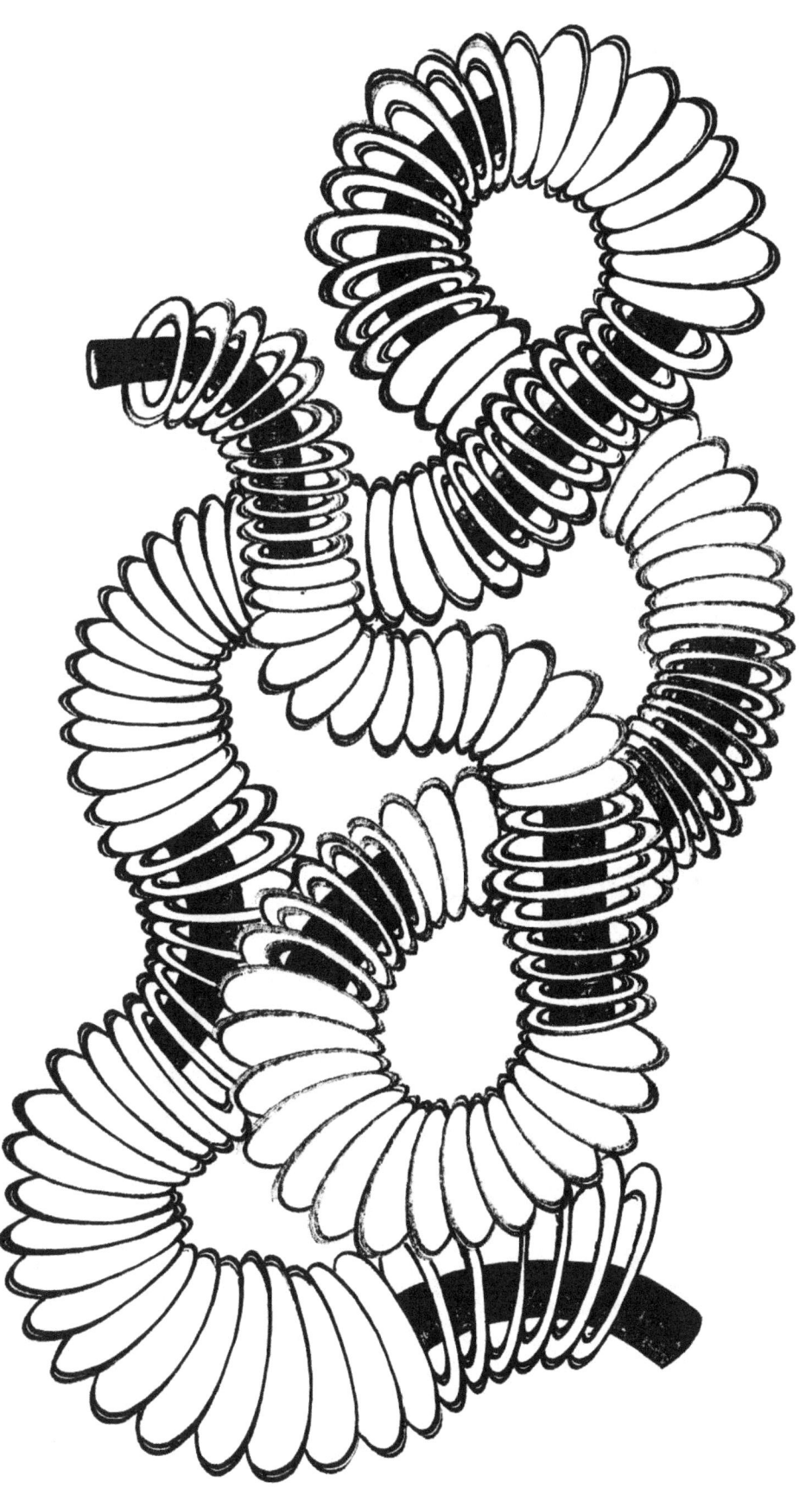

Forgive many things in others; nothing in yourself.

When about to commit a base deed, respect thyself, though there is no witness.

Let us never know what old age is. Let us know the happiness time brings, not count the years.

-- Ausonius (310 AD - 395 AD)

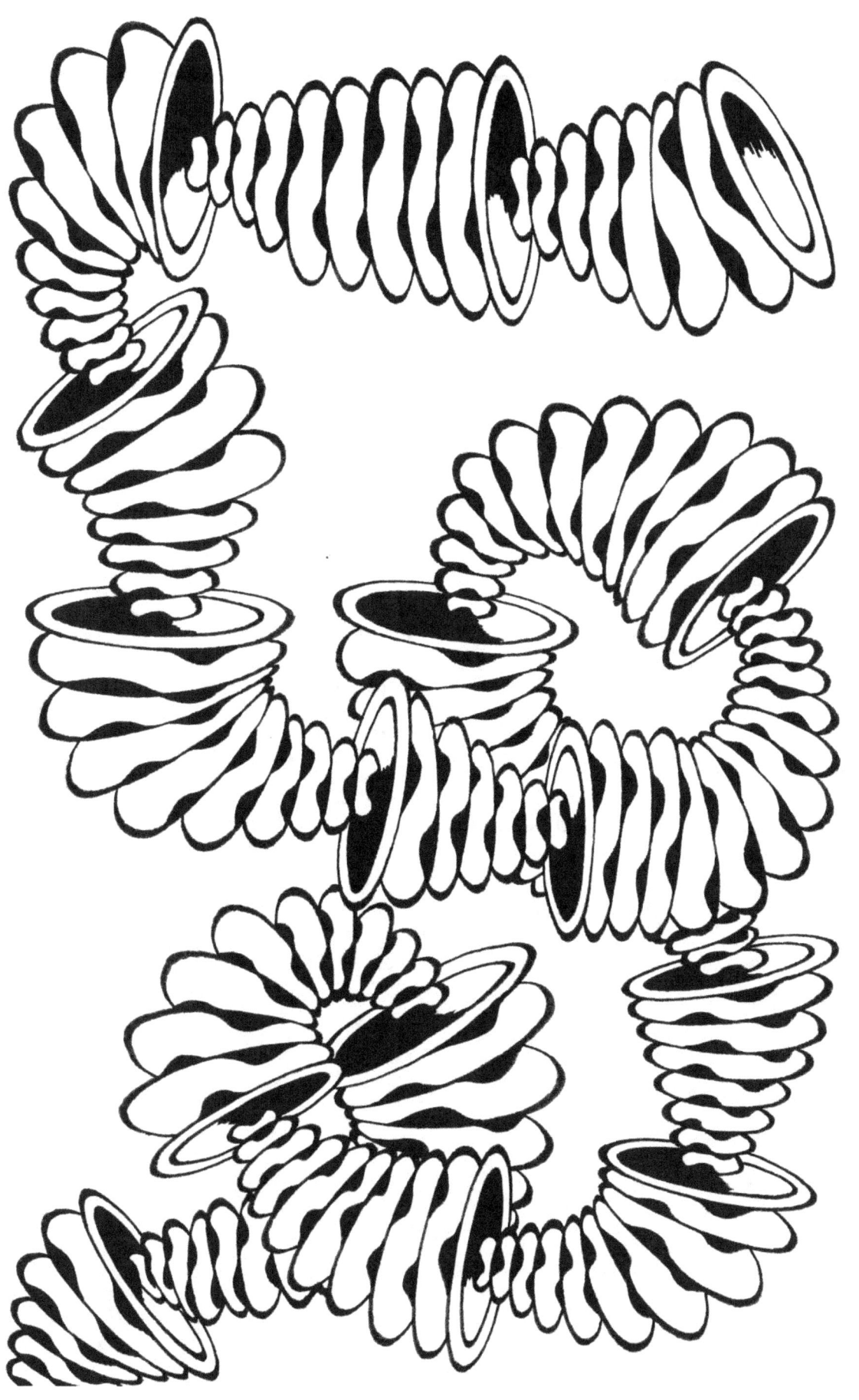

As the blessings of health and fortune have a beginning, so they must also find an end. Everything rises but to fall, and increases but to decay.

Ambition drove many men to become false; to have one thought locked in the breast, another ready on the tongue.

Distinguished ancestors shed a powerful light on their descendants, and forbid the concealment either of their merits or of their demerits.

A good man would prefer to be defeated than to defeat injustice by evil means.

-- Sallust (86 BC – 35 BC)

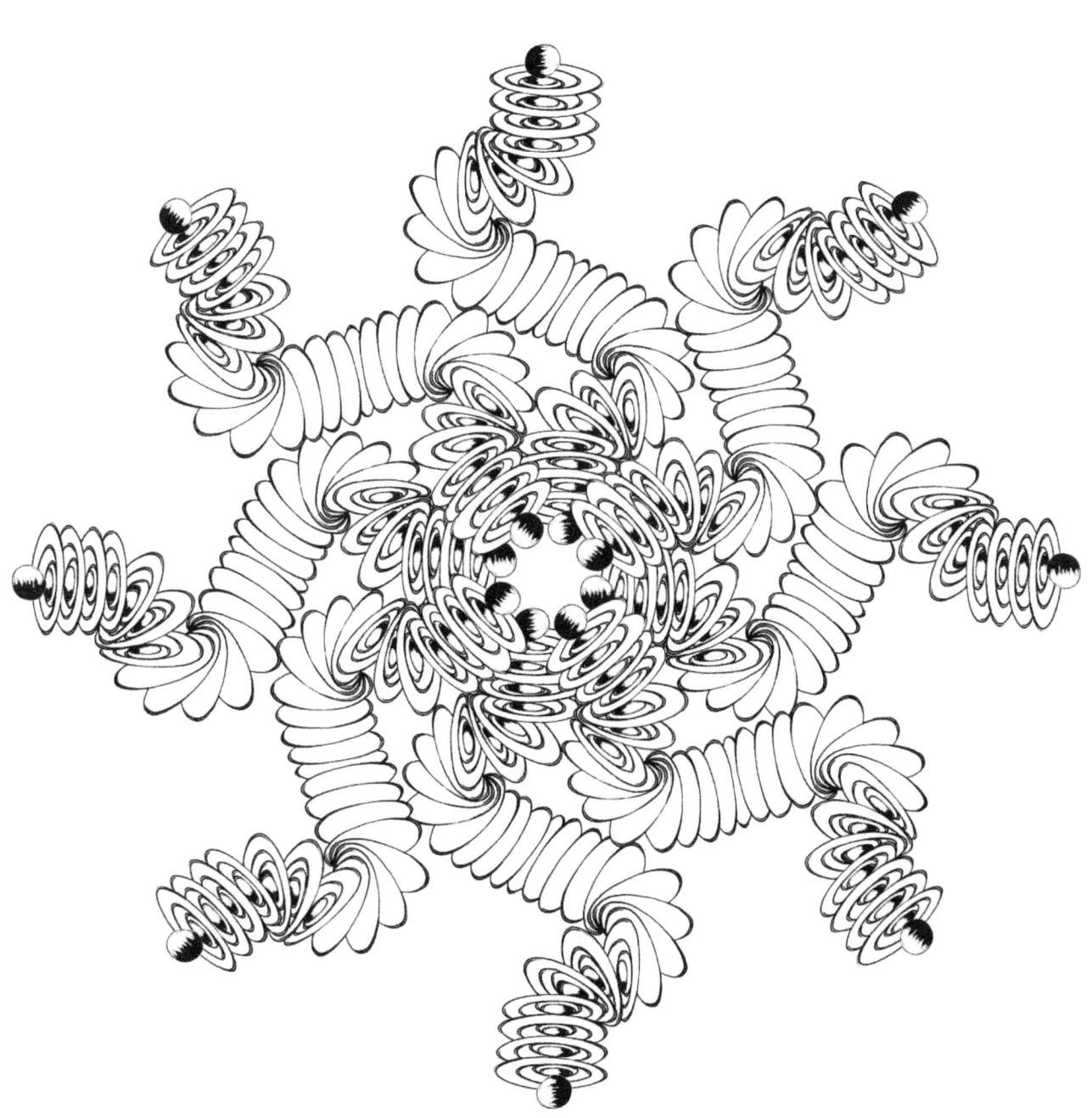

From abundance springs satiety.

Fortune blinds men when she does not wish them to withstand the violence of her onslaughts.

A fraudulent intent, however carefully concealed at the outset, will generally, in the end, betray itself.

All things will be clear and distinct to the man who does not hurry; haste is blind and improvident.

-- Titus Livius (59 BC – 17 AD)

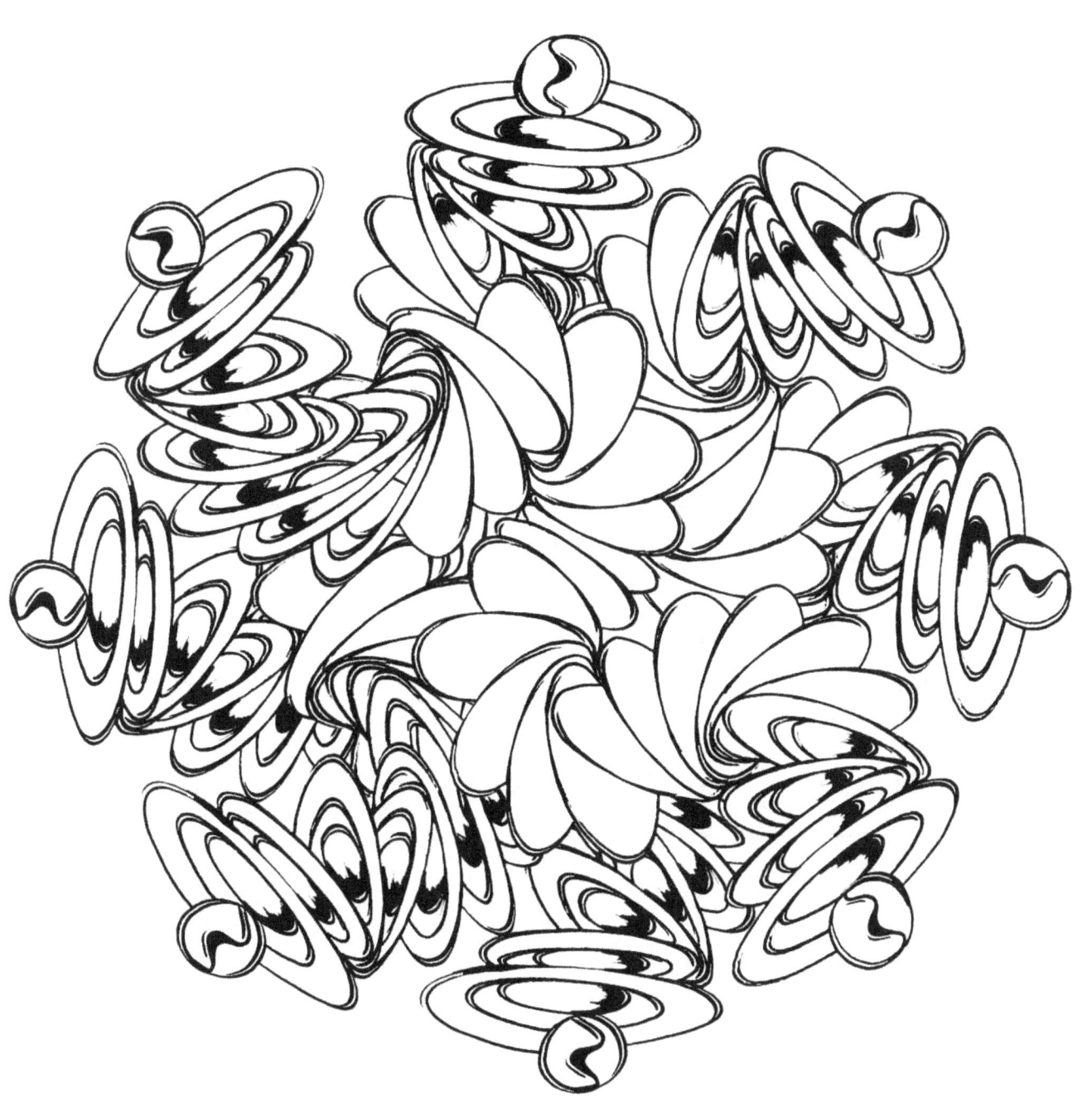

Cowards die many times before their actual deaths.

As a rule, men worry more about what they can't see than about what they can.

It is not these well-fed long-haired men that I fear, but the pale and the hungry-looking.

No one is so brave that he is not disturbed by something unexpected.

The die is cast.

-- Julius Caesar (100 BC – 44 BC)

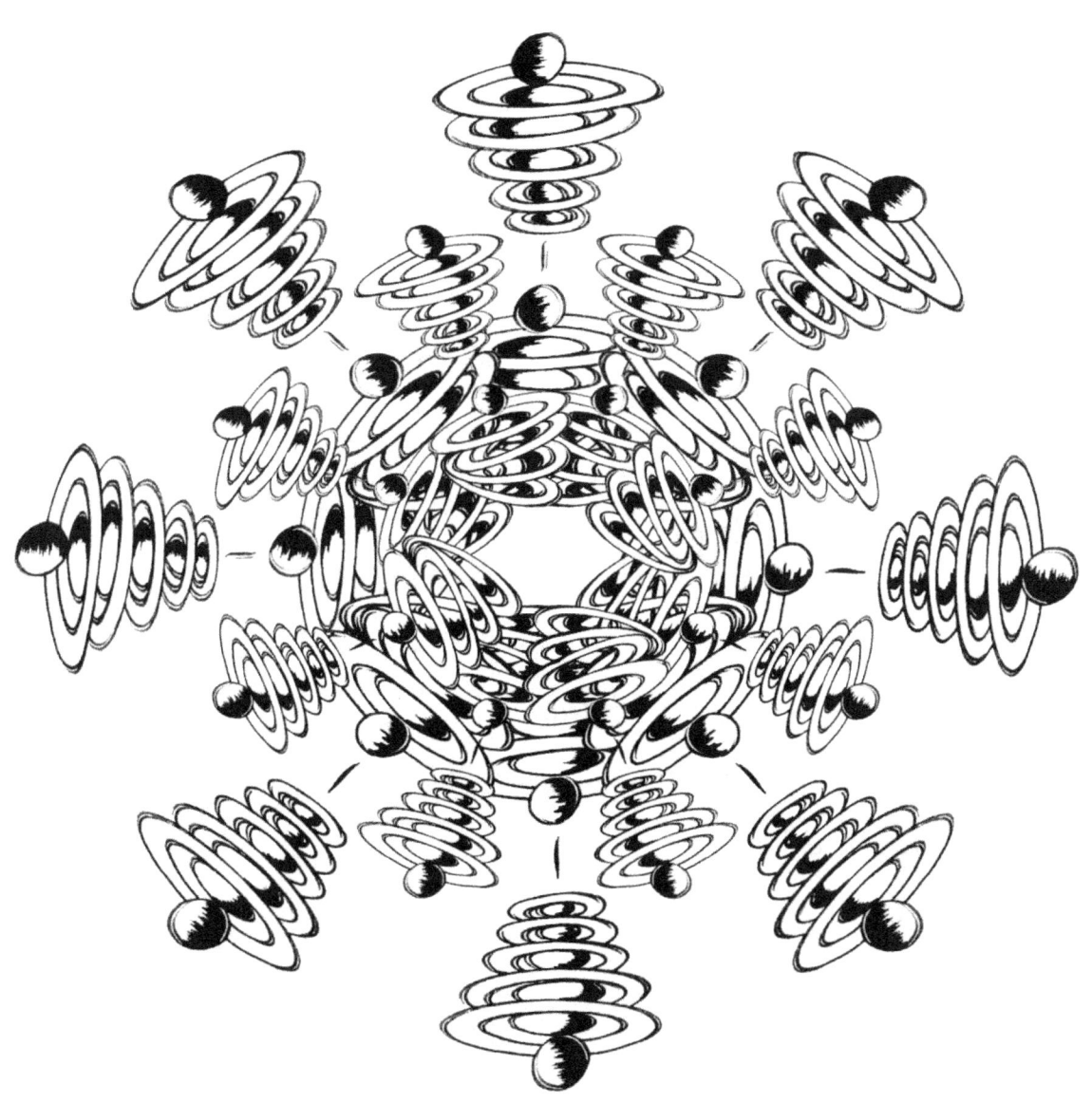

A prince should be slow to punish, and quick to reward.

A new idea is delicate. It can be killed by a sneer or a yawn; it can be stabbed to death by a quip and worried to death by a frown on the right man's brow.

An anthill increases by accumulation. Medicine is consumed by distribution. That which is feared lessens by association. This is the thing to understand.

Time is generally the best doctor.

Time is the devourer of all things.

Time, motion and wine cause sleep.

Use the occasion, for it passes swiftly.

-- Ovid (43 BC – 17 AD)

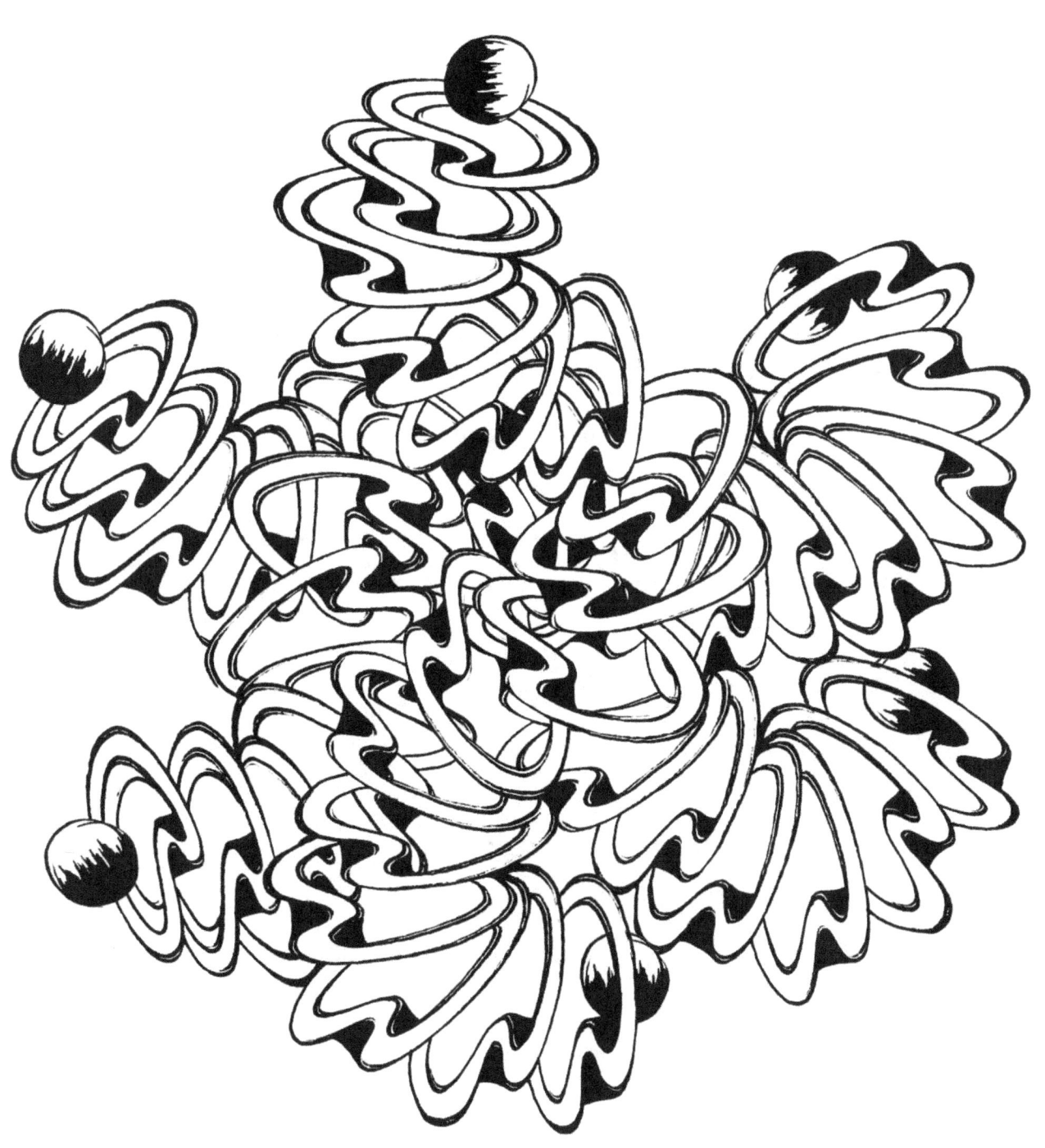

Children should be led into the right paths, not by severity, but by persuasion.

Human nature is so constituted that all see and judge better in the affairs of other men than in their own.

Riches get their value from the mind of the possessor, they are blessings to those who know how to use them and curses to those who do not.

Where there's life, there's hope.

You're a wise person if you can easily direct your attention to whatever needs it.

-- Terence (170 BC – 159 BC)

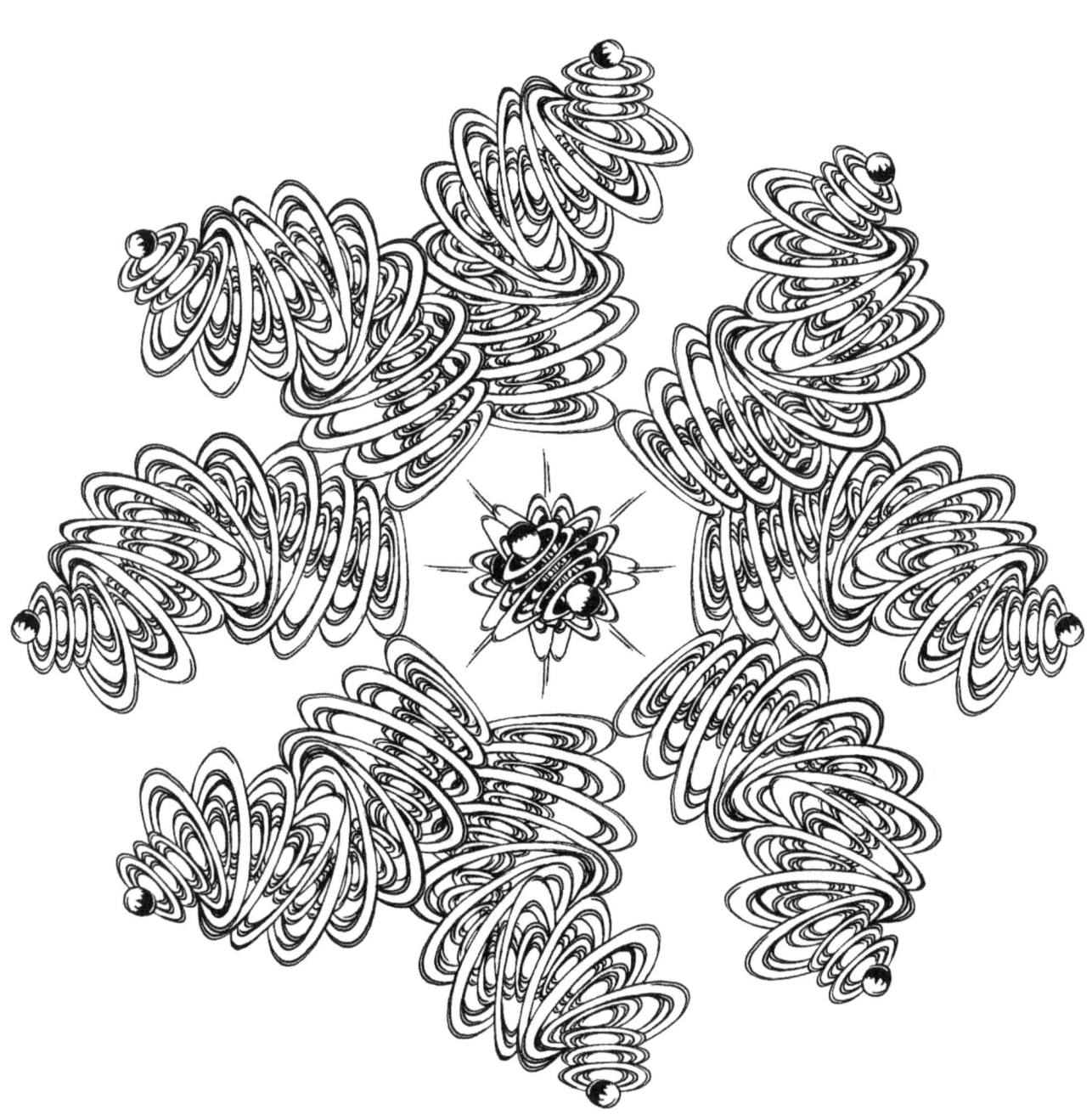

A good reputation is more valuable than money.

An angry father is most cruel towards himself.

Art has a double face, of expression and illusion, just like science has a double face, the reality of error and the phantom of truth.

The happy man is not he who seems thus to others, but who seems thus to himself.

To refuse graciously is to confer a favor.

We die as often as we lose a friend.

-- Publilius Syrus (85 BC – 43 BC)

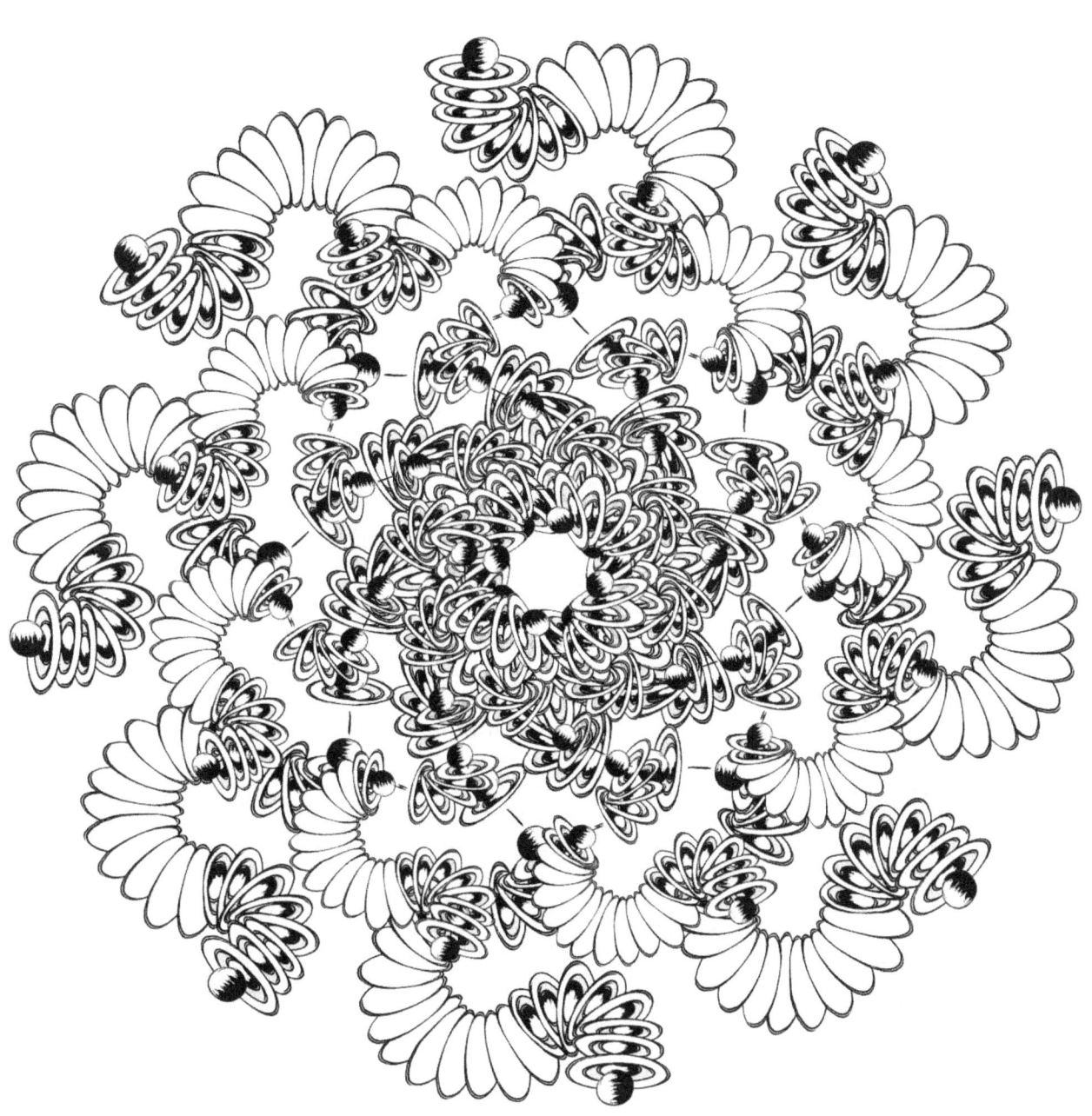

A contented mind is the best source for trouble.

Bad conduct soils the finest ornament more than filth.

Courage is what preserves our liberty, safety, life, and our homes and parents, our country and children. Courage comprises all things.

No guest is so welcome in a friend's house that he will not become a nuisance after three days.

Property is unstable, and youth perishes in a moment. Life itself is held in the grinning fangs of Death, yet men delay to obtain release from the world. Alas, the conduct of mankind is surprising.

The greatest talents often lie buried out of sight.

-- Plautus (254 BC - 184 BC)

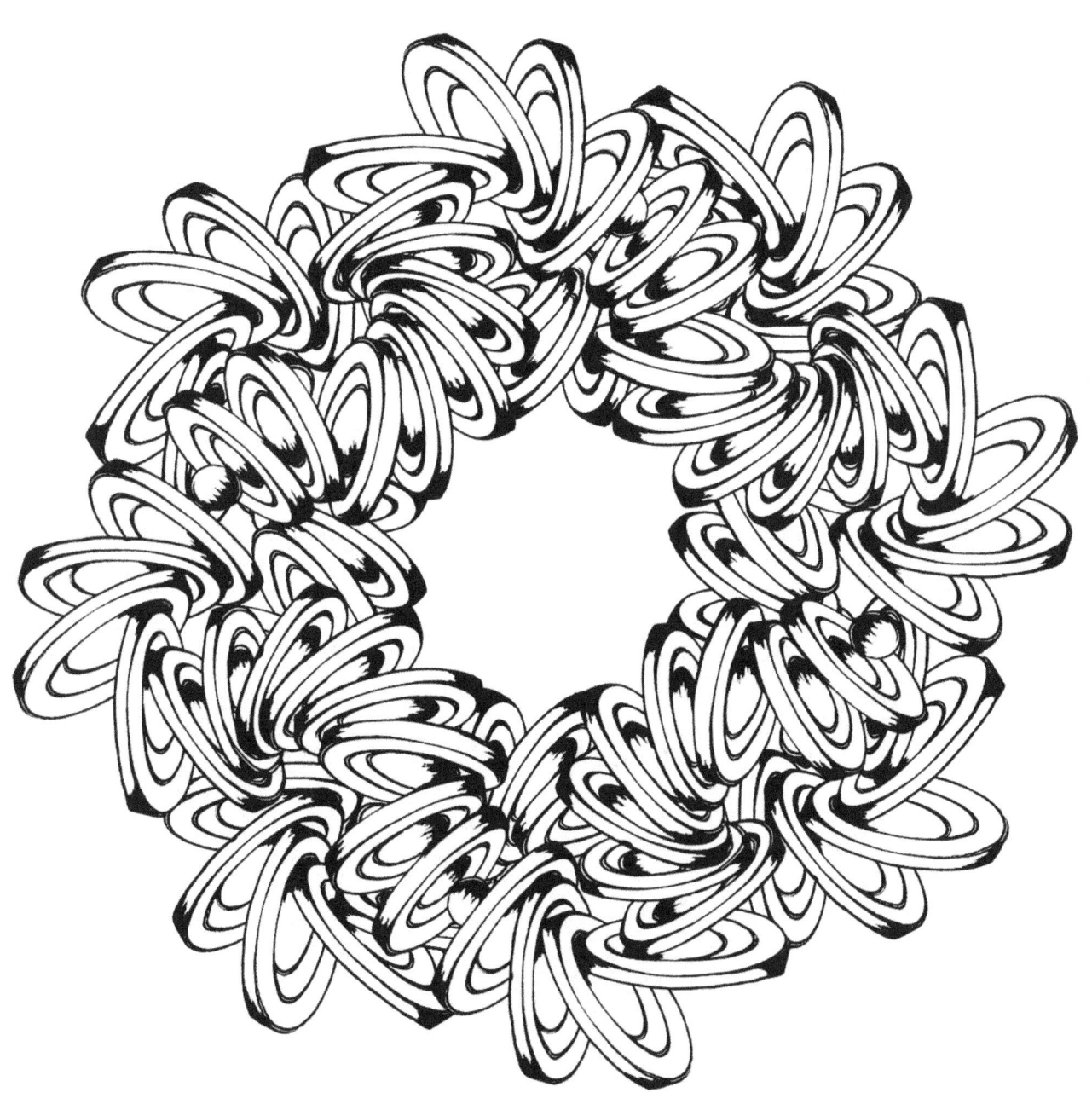

All existing things are really one. We regard those that are beautiful and rare as valuable and those that are ugly as foul and rotten The foul and rotten may come to be transformed into what is rare and valuable, and the rare and valuable into what is foul and rotten.

Cherish that which is within you, and shut off that which is without; for much knowledge is a curse.

Stay centered by accepting whatever you are doing. This is the ultimate.

-- Zhuangzi (4th Century BCE)

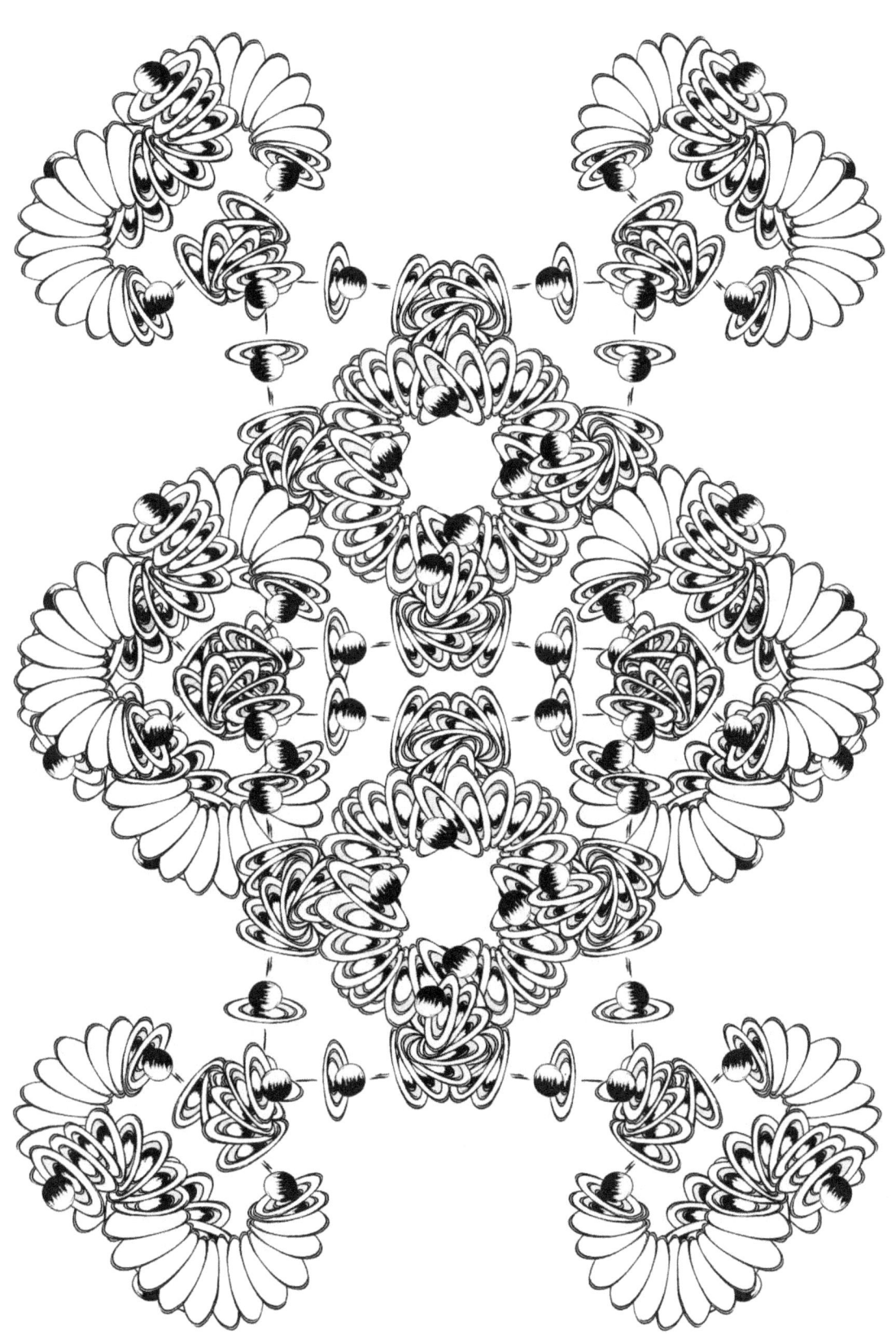

All wrong-doing arises because of mind. If mind is transformed can wrong-doing remain?

An insincere and evil friend is more to be feared than a wild beast; a wild beast may wound your body, but an evil friend will wound your mind.

Better than a thousand hollow words, is one word that brings peace.

Chaos is inherent in all compounded things. Strive on with diligence.

Do not dwell in the past, do not dream of the future, concentrate the mind on the present moment.

Do not overrate what you have received, nor envy others. He who envies others does not obtain peace of mind.

*-- **Buddha (563 BC – 483 BC)***

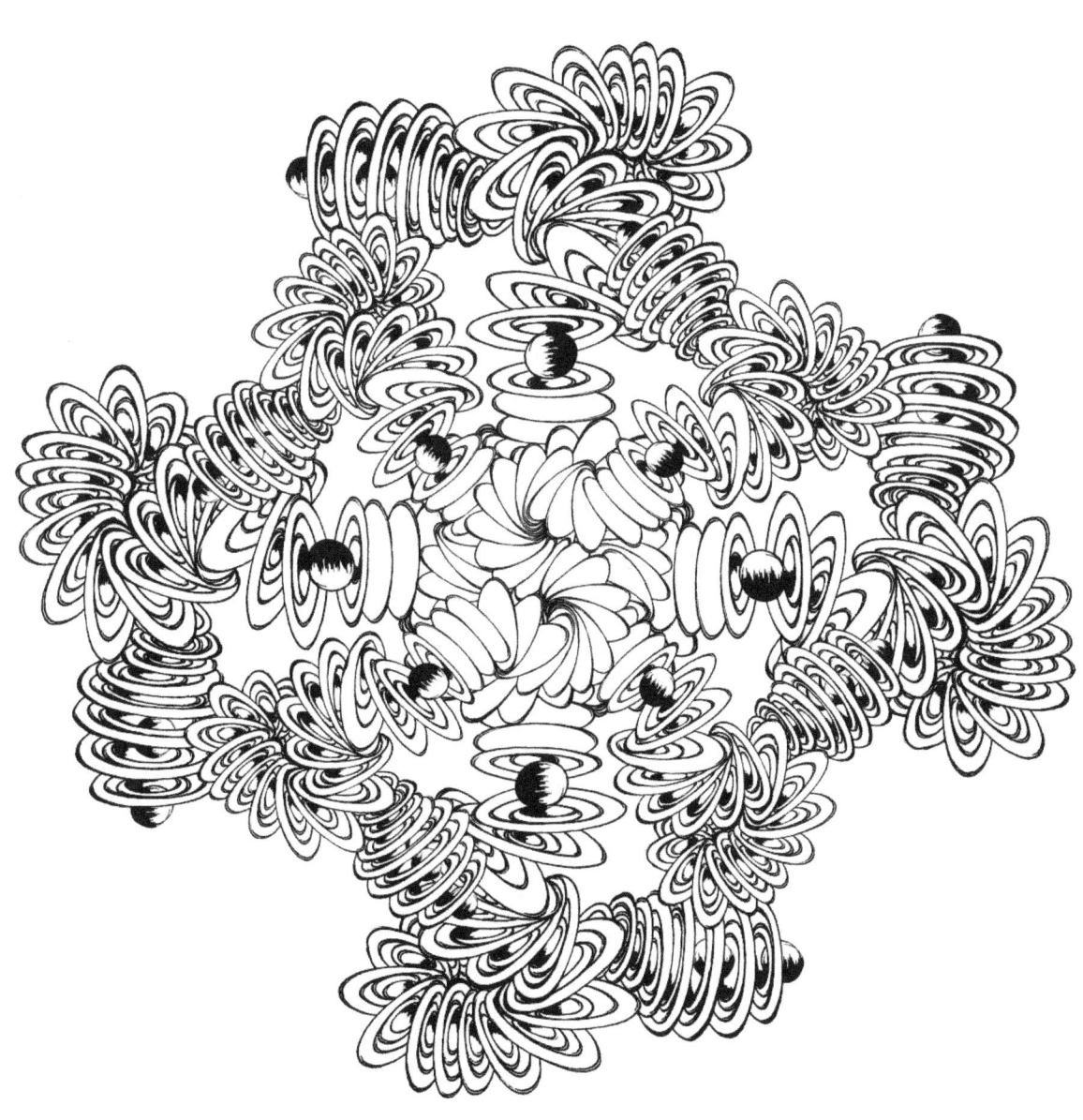

Love hate, not war.

-- *Argo Ink (1964 – present)*

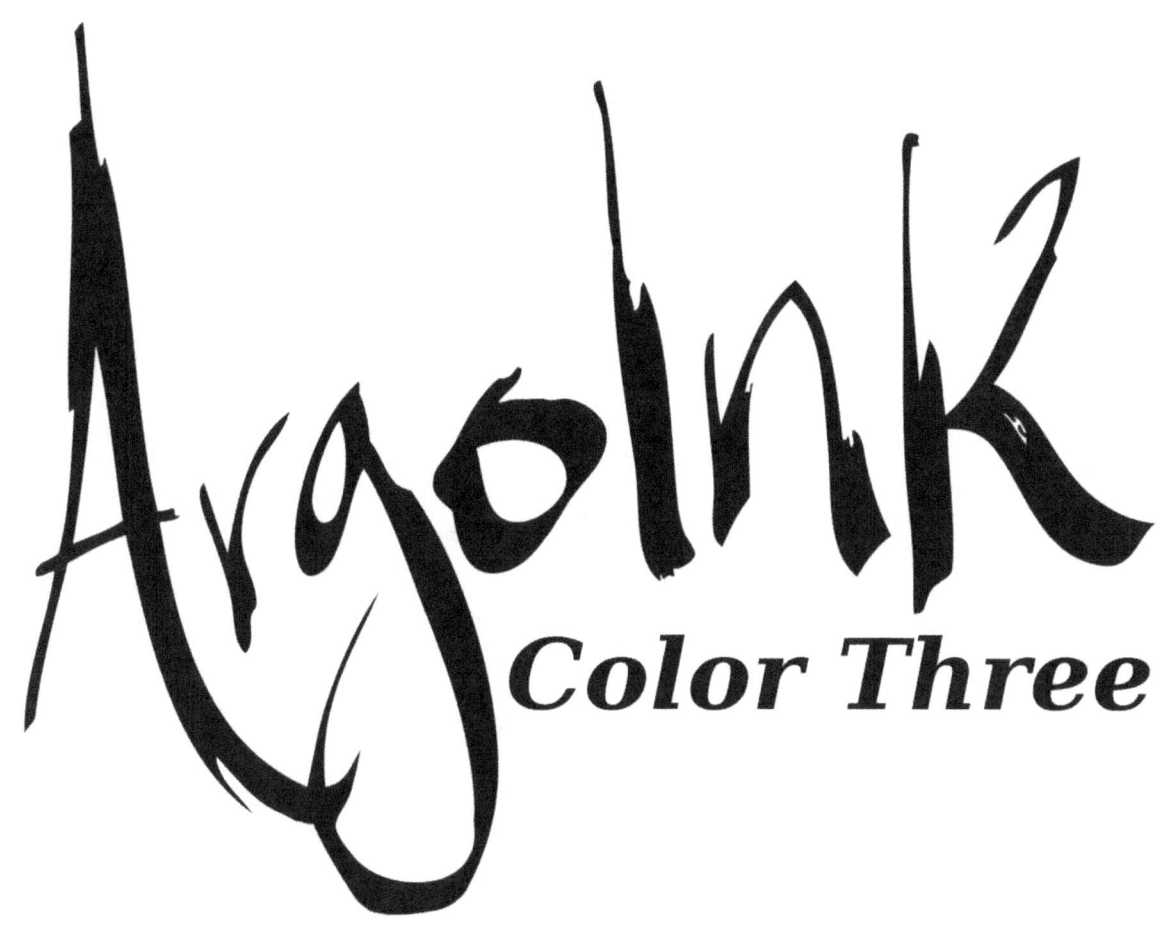

All ArgoInk products are available at 50% off their normal retail price when purchased for school and charitable fundraising events.

Please visit our web site for more details.

www.ArgoInk.com